SAVING THE LAKE

AT

BOBBY HICKS PARK

ODIE JONES, JR.

PUBLISHER: STORYLINE PUBLISHING, L.L.C.

TAMPA, FLORIDA

Library of Congress Control Number: 2017903587

ISBN: 978-0-9979373-0-5

Editor: Gwendolyn Hayes

Published by: Storyline Publishing, L.L.C.

Printed in the United States of America

CONTENTS

PROLOGUE

The Gandy Civic Association (GCA) is located at 4207 W. Oklahoma Ave., Tampa, FL 33615 and is the home of the Sun Bay South neighborhood which is situated in the South Tampa region of the City of Tampa (COT), FL. It was established in 1956 and registered as a Florida nonprofit corporation in 1973.

The purpose of the GCA is to protect and promote the welfare of the area it serves; to provide a forum where residents may hear and be heard in all matters pertaining to any civic concern; to also work with other such organizations and government agencies for the betterment of the community, the City and the State. Accordingly, the facilities and grounds of the association may be used for civic activities such as voting, scouting programs, neighborhood watch, and other similar activities as approved by the association membership.

The area of responsibility is bounded on the north by the south side of Gandy Boulevard, on the east, up to but not including MacDill Avenue, on the south by the north side of Interbay Boulevard, west to Manhattan Avenue and north to Everett Street, then west to Old Tampa Bay.

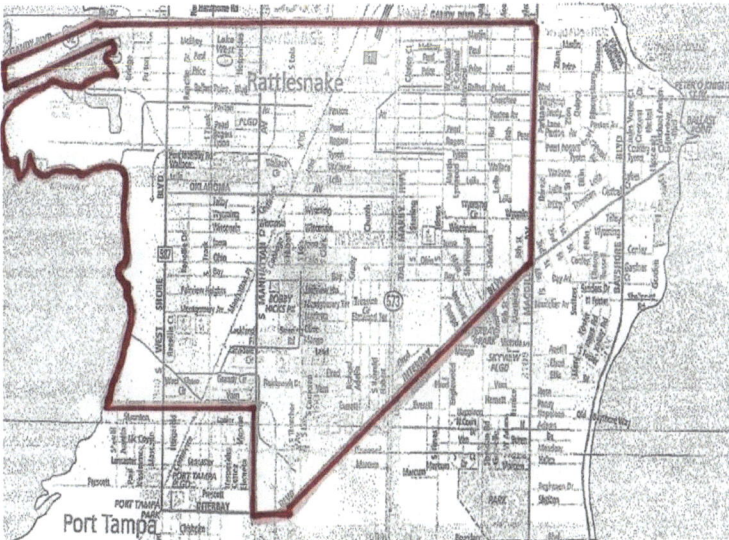

GCA Area of Responsibility in red.

PURPOSE

The purpose of this book is to chronicle information about an important lake which became infested with the aquatic plant known as hyacinths. It is unknown as to how the weed got started in the lake and why it was not attended to sooner. We doubt if those two questions will ever be answered. This is about the efforts of an entire Tampa community, Sun Bay South coming together to solve a very agonizing and difficult problem which affects numerous individuals. This composition is meant to be informational, educational and entertaining. It should inspire every citizen to be alert to situations they think might be detrimental to our natural resources and take actions to solve the problem. The idiom, "An ounce of prevention is worth a pound of cure" certainly applies here. In line with being good citizens, we have tried to accomplish a public service while maintaining cordial public relations and without *ruffling a lot of feathers.*

SPECIAL THANKS

I wish to give special thanks to Mrs. Laura Roake for her bravery in leading an attempt by the South Tampa Survivors to manually remove hyacinths from the Bobby Hicks Lake. This was the start of something big.

Special thanks also to Ms. Tracy Norman, Change.org for leading an Environmental Petition to "Clean up Bobby Hicks Pond." For sure the petition reached far and wide.

Special thanks to Mr. John Dellaquilla for his stedfast loyalty and devotion to the project. His determination to see the mechanical harvester operate properly never waivered.

I want to personally thank Mr. Alan Steenson, President, Gandy Civic Association for his resolute support of Sun Bay South and this project. He has stood shoulder-to-shoulder with me throughout this endeavor.

Thanks to My Jones Family. You are the backbones of all of my accomplishments.

To my daughter Deidre. Thank you for your inspiration, stamina and immeasurable productivity.

ACKNOWLEDGEMENTS

Dick Larosa
Elijah Hall
Elizabeth Behrman
Emily Hone
Humberto Gonzalez
Iva Carter
John Grimsley
Karrel Buck
Pete Stucke
Thomas Mitchell
Tracy Jones
Vivian Hart

CHAPTER 1   -- PARK RENOVATIONS

Someone once said, the best way to tell a good story is to start at the beginning. The beginning is probably that through research, we found a couple of very inspirational newspaper articles. The first was titled, "Bobby Hicks Park Renovations to Hook Families on Fishing" by Orval Jackson of the Tampa Tribune, Saturday, July 29, 2000. Mr. Jackson wrote: "Fishing as a family sport is the aim of a joint effort by state and city agencies at Bobby Hicks Park. A boat ramp for small boats, a fishing pier, and shoreline enhancement are improvements in the works for the pond at Bobby Hicks Park near Robinson High School. The 25-acre pond off Manhattan and Mango Avenues is in the Florida Urban Fishery Project of the Florida Fish and Wildlife Conservation Commission in partnership with the City of Tampa Parks Department. Paul W. Thomas, project leader for the state agency, said its crew will install the boat ramp, pilings and stringers for the pier, and fish feeders, and stock the pond with fish as needed. The rest of the pier will be completed by the Safari Club International, which has donated $5,000 for materials."

"The parks department will be responsible for providing a road into the park, parking, removal of invasive plants and other improvement of conditions along the banks of the pond, restrooms, and overall maintenance...." "The pond at Bobby Hicks Park was created in the early 1960s, when crews removed dirt for construction projects at MacDill (AFB). While digging, they hit a fresh water spring that filled the pit. In the late 1960s, the area was designated as Bobby Hicks Park in honor of the former outdoors editor who became sports editor of the Tampa Tribune. Bobby Hicks Pool later was constructed across from Robinson, but the surrounding area was left untended and virtually unused."

COMMUNITY FOCUS

SouthTampa

Saturday, July 29, 2000
The Tampa Tribune
"Bobby Hicks Park Reno-
vations to Hook Families
on Fishing"

Orval Jackson
(813) 286-0838

CANDACE C. MUNDY/Tribune photo from Eagle 8

This is an aerial view of Bobby Hicks Park and the 25-acre, L-shaped pond that borders it. The pond, already home to
bluegill, largemouth bass, snook, Nile perch and channel catfish, will be stocked with another 2,500 catfish.

**An aerial view of the Bobby Hicks Park & Lake,
Tampa, FL**

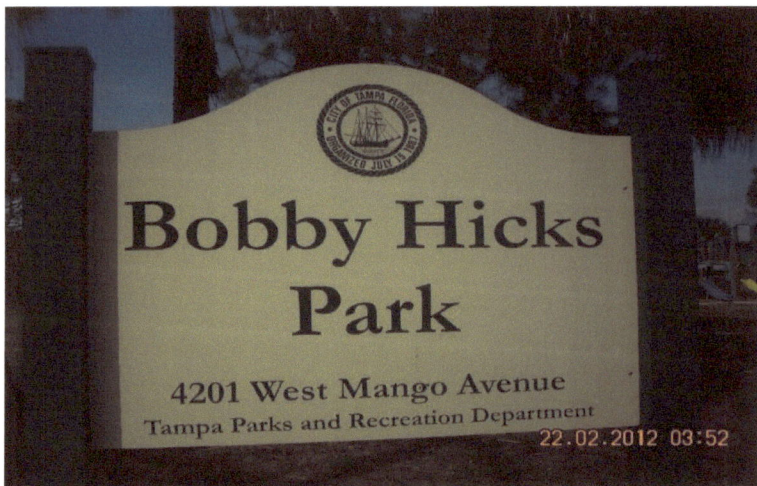

This sign stands on the east side of Bobby Hicks Park, Tampa, FL.

Bobby Hicks Lake, Tampa, FL
(Photo by Karrel Buck, 9 Nov 08)

CHAPTER 2 -- BUILDING THE PIER

The second newspaper article we read was called "Club Hooks Fishing Pier for Park" by Jay Cridlin of the St. Petersburg Times, published June 21, 2002. Mr. Cridlin pretty much confirmed some of Mr. Jackson's writings. Mr. Cridlin wrote: …"The Safari Club, a big-game hunting club that pays huge fees to hunt exotic animals around the globe, built the pier in conjunction with the Fish and Wildlife Conservation Commission as part of an effort to lure fishermen to the park. 'We have a saying in the business,' said Paul Thomas, the urban ponds project manager. 'If you build it, they will come.' The commission created blueprints for the pier and paid about $6,500 to put in the pilings, and the Safari Club ponied up $5,000 to buy the wood. About 25 club members spent about a day building it to specifications – about $12,000 worth of labor, Thomas estimates."

The Safari Club members didn't just decide in one day to build the pier. The reasoning went a little further than 'we got the money, let's spend it.' The FWC was already carrying a traveling supply of fishing equipment for the public so the Safari Club donated a trailer to store it in. According to the St. Pete Times article, "At the dedication, 75 childeren from the on-site Boys and Girls Club and Mangrove Marcus day camp were loaned rods and reels from the trailer to test out the new pier. "It's nice because you don't have to trudge through the mud and everything to get here," said 11-year old Blake Petty, a Mangrove Marcus camper. Commission spokesman Gary Morse said the pier will give children a chance to interact with nature.

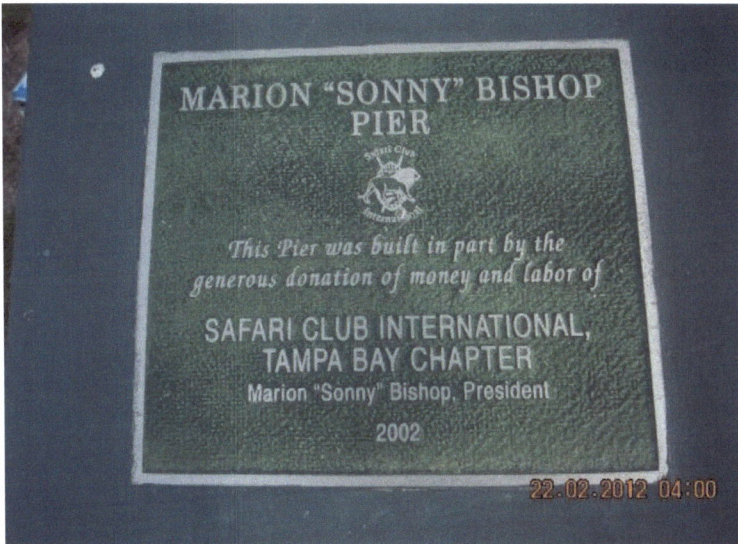

**The above sign is posted near the pier at
Bobby Hicks Park, Tampa, FL**

**The 170-foot long Marion "Sonny" Bishop Pier was built in
2002 (Photo by Odie Jones, Jr., 4 May 12).**

"These kids, particularly in an urban environment, are not really

having a lot of contact with the outdoors, and the concept of conservation", he said. "It's a perfect spot to put a fishing pier and educate people to those values."

Bobby Hicks Lake & Pier, Tampa, FL
(Photo by Karrel Buck, 9 Nov 08).

CHAPTER 3 -- OUR BEAUTIFUL POND

When my family and I moved to West Bay Avenue in South Tampa, the lake at Bobby Hicks Park was stunningly beautiful – gleaming crisp and clear. We wondered why the brush on the western boundary was not cleared away so we in the neighborhood could claim *lake front property.* The truth is, I actually did call the COT Public Works Department and within a couple of hours, several workers were dispatched to clear away the overgrowth. Unfortunately for the residents on West Bay, a prominent city official showed up almost immediately claiming the entire lake area was designated as an official animals, birds and plants sanctuary. We asked the city councilwoman (unnamed) to just show us an inkling of evidence to that fact. We don't know if she had got the word that a "stand your ground" law was heading to Tampa Bay but she stood her ground and said, "No more cutting in this area or someone is going to be paying a big fat fine!" There went our *lake front property!*

Beautiful Bobby Hicks Lake, Tampa, FL
(Photo by Karrel Buck, 9 Nov 08).

For over 30 years that we know of, the folks in Sun Bay South enjoyed the priviledge of fishing at the Bobby Hicks Lake. Although there were suggestions made by neighbors to the original planners that there should be playground equipment and a picnic area, the idea never materialized. Still, everyone went to the park and enjoyed fishing. Our oldest son was a student at Robinson High School and one of the most frequent visitors there. He often talked about the variety of fish in the lake; proving it by bringing home a fine mess of fish. My youngest son also attended Robinson and had told tall fish tales to his two young sons. Just by chance, I met a man named Bob Seville who said he lived at Ballast Point. He too related to me that when he attended Robinson High School, he and friends would fish and also swim in a crystal clear Bobby Hicks Lake. There were so many fishy stories that I just couldn't seem to keep up with them all.

Photographer Karrel Buck published an album of photos of the Bobby Hicks Park. She included photos of the beautiful lake with its birds and she wrote, "...Lucky me, I have a nice bird sanctuary in my backyard." She must have known the city councilwoman I encountered earlier.

Birds taking sanctuary at Bobby Hicks Lake.
(Photo by Karrel Buck, August 2, 2009).

CHAPTER 4 -- THE AQUATIC WEED – HYACINTHS

My youngest son wanted to know what happened to the lake. He and the boys were anxious to get to the lake and try their hands at fishing when they came home in 2011. Guess what? They were thoroughly disappointed and I was super embarassed that the once lively waterway and fishing mecca looked like an unkept swamp. We ended up at Ballast Point catching a few thorny catfish. He asked, "What caused the lake to become overrun with weeds?" Obviously, I could not provide an answer. I told them what I told Mr. Thomas Mitchell, neighbor, we will do whatever we can to get the lake cleaned up. The hyacinths in the Bobby Hicks Lake is an ugly anomaly.

There are other neighbors who have openly expressed their concerns. For example, soon after I had finished photographing from various positions across the lake, I was accosted by Mrs. Aida Berrera and Ms. Edna Jensen. They expressed outrage over, as they put it, "Someone allowing the lake to deteriorate to such dispicable state." They seemed put at ease when I told them of my plans to bring the matter before the Gandy Civic Association (GCA). I kept my promise at our next general meeting. GCA President, Mr. Alan "AL" Steenson and the members were so receptive to my idea that they put me in charge of what they called, "Saving the lake."

This is a view of the Bobby Hicks Lake after the hyacinths began to turn brown. (Photo by Odie Jones, Jr. 22 Feb 12).

Hyacinths starting to bloom at Bobby Hicks Lake, Tampa, FL (Photo by Odie Jones, Jr., 4 May 12).

CHAPTER 5 -- A MANUAL COMMUNITY EFFORT

Obviously, GCA members cared about Bobby Hicks Park as far back as the year 2000. When Mr. Orval Jackson wrote the Tampa Tribune article, "Bobby Hicks Park Renovations to Hook Families on Fishing," GCA President Joe Marchitto was quoted as saying, "It's about time, They're going to really use it, I know they will."

Before I got involved with restoring the lake, there had been a manual cleanup effort by Mrs. Laura Roake, member of South Tampa Survivors, and 50 to 75 other citizens. She coordinated through an organization called TampaBeautiful.org and the COT. On April 23, 2011, the group gathered at Bobby Hicks Park with rakes, hoes, forks, buckets, wheel barrels and anything else they could use to untangle and remove the hyacinths from the shoreline. City workers provided a payloader and a dump truck to haul the weed away. Mrs. Roake recalled that the attempt at manually removing the hyacinths was one of the most difficult and backbreaking challenges they could have ever taken on. It was dirty, messy and unrewarding because as they hauled out one plant, there appeared to be two more taking its place right before their eyes. The job was so overpowering that it was terminated after one day. They were promised that the city would continue the job with the proper equipment.

South Tampa Survivors And other Sun Bay South neighbors manually removing water hyacinths from the Bobby Hicks Lake (Photo by Laura Roake, 23 Apr 11).

Sun Bay South Citizens Manually Removing The Hyacinths From Bobby Hicks Lake. (Photo by Laura Roake, 23 Apr 11).

A COT Parks & Rec. employee uses a payloader to load hyacinths into a dump truck for hauling away. The pesty weed was manually pulled from the Bobby Hick Lake by citizens of Sun Bay South. (Photo by Laura Roake, 23 Apr 11).

CHAPTER 6 -- DON'T SPRAY THE LAKE

GCA's latest campaign to do the cleanup actually began in February 2012 and after I had snapped some pictures of the hyacinths covered lake. There had been lots of communications passed back and forth. We communicated with numerous people in person, via the telephone, and through emails. This includes the concerned citizens as well as interested government officials.

I had a telephone conversation with Mr. John Grimsley, COT Parks & Rec South Area Supervisor. I explained to him that I was a member of the GCA and had observed the overgrown condition of the lake; and that we were very interested in helping to do whatever we could to restore the lake to its pristine condition. He was very receptive to my call and proceeded to fill me in on their on-going operations to take care of the lake. According to him, the lake is periodically being *sprayed*, depending on the wind and other weather related factors. "There are alligators and other wildlife to consider therefore, the notion of applying enough chemicals to remove or kill the pesky plant quickly is out of the question. Too much chemicals could kill the lake. A while ago, people from the neighborhood joined in to help city workers manually remove some of the plant but that amounted to little or no improvement considering the size of the lake and how fast the plant grows" he explained. He said, "There are numerous methods of solving the problem. The most effective method is to employ a harvester; however, it is also the most costly."

During coffee with Hillsborough County Commissioner (HCCOMM) Sandra Murman, District 1, at Nola's Café, Tampa, FL, March 16, 2012, I was allowed to present our concerns along with the pictures I had taken of the lake. I told her that the GCA wanted to know if there was anything that her office could do to help us out. She expressed an eagerness to look into the problem since, as she pointed out, it is within her district. I also explained

29

that we were aware of the financial crunch caused by the slow economy, still we could best benefit from financial aid. She said she wanted the Environmental Protection Commissin (EPC) of Hillsborough County to get involved but in the meantime, she would look into the possibility of providing some funding if needed.

During the week of March 28, 2012, Mr. Richard Boler, HCEPC telephoned me to say he was calling at the request of Comm. Murman. He said he had spoken with Mr. Grimsley who told him basically the same thing Mr. Grimsley told me earlier; that they were slowly spraying the lake with little or no effect. He said he also talked to Mr. Carlos Fernandez, Director of HC Mosquito Control. Mr. Fernandez told him that because they are so involved with mosquito control, it is almost impossible to allow their equipment to be used for anything else. After my conversation with Mr. Boler, I called Mr Grimsley again. He said he had spoken to a couple of officials, but didn't get any further due to there being little money. He said he would continue to seek answers to the hyacinths problem.

As I was surfing the internet for help during the first week of April, 2012, I came across pages and pages of information under the heading, "Plant Management in Florida Waters: An Integrated Approach." I couldn't help but notice the sub-title, "Citizens," which I will quote in part: "Not only do local, state and federal governments have a responsibility to protect our natural environments, but it is also our duty as Florida citizens to take the initiative to do things within our powers that will contribute to the betterment of our local habitats." Another sub-title, "Control Methods," really caused me to sit up and take note. It read in part: "Approximately $60 million annually (2008) is spent by state agencies, the federal government, water management districts, counties and cities to manage invasive plants in Florida's lakes, rivers, canals, marshes and swamps." After reading the above information, the most pressing question then was, how much financing can we get to manage the invasive water hyacinths in our lake at Bobby Hicks Park, Tampa, FL? This prompted a letter to Florida State Representative (Rep.) Dana Young in the hope of getting some help out of Tallahassee. We figured that if we were searching in the wrong place for a solution to our problem, surely the state would point us in the right direction. If they couldn't help us, then maybe Rep. Young would tell us who to turn to. Sadly to say, and for some unknown reason, we did not get a response.

On the other hand, we did get some advice; mainly from people with pools in their back yards. A suggestion came from one of our GCA members, Mr. John Stearnes who said to simply use carp fish to devour the plant. True, biological control includes the use of Chinese grass carp, a fish from China which is one of the most effective agents for hydrilla and some other aquatic plants. Unfortunately, the fish does not eat only hydrilla; it will consume most submerged and emerged aquatic plants once hydrilla is depleted. Also, there is no efficient way to recapture the carp and this limits the feasibility of using them.

A report by the North American Lake Management Society, titled, "Lake and Reservoir Management: Practical Applications, 1985" revealed: "...Use of grass carp in various parts of the United States has been restricted or forbidden (for example Florida) because various studies have suggested that grass carp can increase lake eutrophication and cause changes in the tropic status (Opuszynski, 1972, 1979)."

Al Steenson forwarded an email to me from HCComm. Kevin Beckner, District 6, in which the Commissiner wrote, "Go Green on Earth Day, April 22, 2012." As Chairman, HCEPC, he offered tips on how to "Go Green," e.g. "Volunteering to clean our beaches, roadways and parks." I sent the Comm. an email thanking him for his flyer and asked for his help in cleaning up our Bobby Hicks Park Lake. His Legislative aide, Ms. Holly East responded in an email that our case ID45089 had been assigned to Senior Administrative Specialist Joyce Moore who would contact me. Ms. East went on to say, "Commissiner Beckner has had some success with asking the EPC to eliminate invasive plants by spraying them and he hopes that they can do this with hyacinths." I forwarded the email to President Steenson and he and I readily agreed that we didn't want the lake sprayed for fear of giving it a chemical death. We believed that the indiscriminate use of herbicides could choke the lake; causing prolonged stagnation.

I called Comm. Beckner's office on May 4, 2012 and spoke with Renee, asking that they do not use spray to clean up the lake. On Wednesday, May 9, 2012, I received a phone call from Mr. Tom Ash, Environmental Restoration, Water Management Division, HCEPC. He said he was calling in reference to Case ID45089 having to do with the Bobby Hicks Park Lake. We discussed the use of mechanical, biological, and chemical methods to control the hyacinths but agreed neither of us knew enough about aquatic plant management to reach a useful decision. He said he had spoken with Mr. John Grimsley of COT Parks & Rec. and felt the situation was being handled by them as best they could. He indicated since his office was not one to actually oversee the cleanup, he would close the case.

Around May 10, 2012, we learned that Mr. Greg Bayor was the new Director of the COT Parks & Rec. Dept. In talking with Mr. John Grimsley, we asked about a water quality test. He stated he had been in the job for four years but didn't know if there had been one or not. He said he had been looking into the purchase of a small harvester but was skeptical due to the high cost; about $70-80,000. He felt the water hyacinths may have been transplanted at the lake by an enthusiastic plant lover who was unaware of the possible adverse consequences of his or her actions. We asked about where the Bobby Hicks Pool was being drained and he assured me that it was not going into the lake. I told Mr. Grimsley about my visit to the nearby Gadsden Park Lake near MacDill AFB and how refreshing it was to see how crystal clear the water was compared to the smothered Bobby Hicks Lake. I asked if he oversaw that lake. He said the Team Supervisor for Gadsden Park was Mr. John Allen. I revisited Gadsden Park and the maintenance men there said they regularly clean the area and there was never any hyacinths in the Gadsden Lake.

Lively Gadsden Park Lake, Tampa, FL with its cool, clear water.

**Stifled Bobby Hicks Park Lake with its pesty
hyacinths aquatic weeds.**

It is difficult to believe that the Gadsden Park Lake and the

Bobby Hicks Lake are parts of the same Tampa Bay Urban

Fishery Project.

On May 18, 2012, Mr. Richard "Dick" Larosa, a concerned

citizen wrote a very strongly worded email to the office of

HCComm. District 1, Sandra Murman. Her Legislative Aide,

Ms. Della Cury wrote back, "Mr. Larosa, We met with Al

Steenson and Odie Jones this morning with Commissioner

Murman. We are pursuing various avenues of clean-up while Mr. Jones waits for a response from Mr. Allen at the City. I will forward your email to your City Councilman, Harry Cohen and will copy you on any answers we receive regarding our clean-up efforts. Thank you for taking the time to write."

CHAPTER 7 -- ASK CITY HALL

A newspaper article appeared in the Tampa Tribune on June 12, 2012 entitled, "Mayor, Slash City park fees." We quickly drafted a letter to the mayor stating he had been quoted as saying, "Our parks are the foundation of our strength as a city. I want those parks to be welcoming and user-friendly for residents and nonresidents alike." Along with pictures of the Bobby Hicks Park Lake and the Gadsden Park Lake, we wrote, "We feel that accelerated cleanup of this important lake would certainly enhance your parks program and prove that we in *Sun Bay South* do matter." Although we didn't hear directly from Mayor Buckhorn, we got an update from Mr. Greg Bayor which we took as a reply to our letter to the mayor. He said he visited the lake shortly after taking office in May and since then they have been formulating a plan of action. He listed three options which he sent to Mayor Buckhorn: (1) chemically treat the lake, (2) purchase a harvester and (3) piggy-back on the contracts of other jurisdictions. We replied to Mr. Bayor's

letter with a bold request, "PLEASE DONOT SPRAY THE LAKE." Wikipedia, the free encyclopedia states, "The application of herbicides for controlling water hyacinths has been carried out for many years and it has been found that there is a good success rate when dealing with small infestations. A main concern when using herbicides is the environmental and health related effects, especially where people collect water for drinking and washing." The way we saw it was we didn't plan to drink the water nor swim in it, but how about the fish? We know they swim but where do they get their drinking water?

We received an email on July 16, 2012 from Mr. Bayor which read, "...Per your wishes and research done by staff here, the concept of spraying the lake is REJECTED!" He went on to write that they have tentative approval to purchase a harvester effective October 1, 2012 (the beginning of the new fiscal year).

He explained that it's a lengthy process of getting the machinery, training, etc. but felt it would be helpful for all the City's lakes and ponds. He said, "Bobby Hicks will come first." While we anticipated the actions by COT Parks & Rec., we continually looked for ways to speedup the process. With respect to a slow economy, we believed cooperation and teamwork was the answer to our community improvement goals. We hoped the City of Tampa, Hillsborough County and the State of Florida could combine their efforts to fix our lake.

FORUM ON BOBBY HICKS PARK AND LAKE

According to a Tampa Tribune newspaper article dated August 1, 2012, "The (Hillsborough County) Commission approved more than $28 million in parks and recreation improvements...."

It only seems right that some of the $28 million should be flagged for us here in South Tampa and our Bobby Hicks Park Lake.

October 1, 2012 seemed like a lifetime away while we were waiting for the COT to act on purchasing the harvester. GCA President Al Steenson was far better informed of the interworkings of city government so he knew that purchasing had to first get on the City Council Agenda. Why? Because they must approve such expensive items. Since we had possibly aided in the rejection of spraying the lake, the least we could do was to watch for a harvester to appear on the agenda and stand before city council to defend it. To that end we had to learn something about mechanical harvesters. Surfing the internet, we found a book with the chapter titled, "Aquatic Plant Management – Mechanical Harvesting" by the Department of Ecology, State of Washington. This book was mostly about the large machines which both cut and collect aquatic plants. Cut plants are removed from the water by a conveyor belt system and stored on the harvester until disposal. A barge may be stationed near the harvesting site for temporary plant storage or the harvester carries the cut weeds to shore. The shore station equipment is usually a shore conveyor that mates to the harvester and lifts the cut plants into a dump truck. Harvested weeds are disposed of in landfills, used as compost, or in reclaiming spent gravel pits or similar sites. According to the book, the disadvantages of using a harvester outweighs the advantages by 10 to 5. Still, harvesting seemed to be the best option for the time being. We at GCA were depending upon the professionals to make the right decision as how to clean Bobby Hicks Lake and we were willing to support them all the way.

From my home, I heard the loud sound of something like heavy equipment being operated in or near the lake. On September 6, 2012, all I could think of was that the COT Parks & Rec. had purchased a harvester and it was being used to clear out the hyacinths. I immediately became all excited over the prospect that the city had acted ahead of schedule to send a little happiness our way in Sun Bay South. Naturally, if so, this was something I had to witness with my own eyes. So, I grabbed my little camera, jumped into my van and raced around the block to the lake.

Hillsborough County Mosquito Control spraying due to the West Nile Virus alert (Photo by Odie Jones, Jr., 6 Sep 12).

What I saw was not a harvester, but a small amphibious vehicle wading through the drainage ditch leading to the lake. The operator held a long wan-like device in one hand which he moved back and forth as it emitted a misty cloud. When he saw me taking pictures, he stopped the vehicle, removed his safety mask and greeted me with a smile. I complimented him on a good job and he eagerly explained that he was spraying the ditch for mosquitos. After which he was to spray the outer banks of the lake to kill the lettuce and hyacinths. At that point my eyes widened and my ears stood up like a bloodhound on the trail of its prey. I asked him how were they getting the spray out to the middle of the lake. About that time, I heard a loud roar like what I had heard from my home. He pointed in the direction of the lake and I could see that another operator was spraying the lake from an airboat.

Hillsborough County Mosquito Control airboat spraying for mosquitos, lettuce and hyacinths (Photo by Odie Jones, Jr., 6 Sep 12.

I went to the other side of the lake to the pier and near the Liberty Mampierre Boys & Girls Club where I could take more photos of the operation. I also wanted to talk to the operator of the airboat but he never came close enough to hear me calling him. The sign on the work truck read: "Mosquito Control."

Mosquito Control Support Vehicles

After I returned home that day, I called Mr. Grimsley. He explained that mosquito control is performed by Hillsborough County and he wasn't aware that they were spraying the lake that day. His guess was that they were reacting to the West Nile Virus alert. He also thought they weren't going to try to kill all of the hyacinths at once but were trying to control the growth as was attempted over the past year or so. I reminded him of Mr.

Bayor's email, "…the concept of spraying the lake is REJECTED!" He said the plan to purchase a harvester was still alive but he believed it would take some time to carry out. With a fairly new COT Mayor and a new Parks & Rec. Director, the Administration showed increased interest in the lake in spite of facing the Republican National Convention and the downtown Tampa Riverwalk project. He also said he didn't think the county operators would do anything to harm the lake. Still we wondered if the herbicide might be ineffective on the mosquitos in the extremely dense hyacinths. On the other hand, we wondered if the spray would kill most of the weeds; causing them to settle to the bottom and eventually kill the lake. I thanked him for his confidence and promised we would stay in touch. We could only wait and see what would happened.

CHAPTER 8 -- THE BIG-TICKET HARVESTER

There is an old saying, "Don't count your chickens before they hatch." Well, we weren't counting chickens; instead, we were crossing our fingers – and for a good reason. I received a telephone call Tuesday, October 16, 2012 from Mr. Grimsley inviting us to attend a demonstration of an aquatic weed harvester at Bobby Hicks Lake on Thursday, October 18, 2012 at 12:30 p.m. I admit I was really surprised; however, I was more elated at the prospects of getting the lake cleared of the hyacinths. Since I had a doctor's appointment at 10:30 a.m., I was somewhat apprehensive that I wouldn't arrive on time. I called Al and guess what? You guessed it, he had an appointment also.

Nevertheless, I arrived at Bobby Hicks Park Lake in ample time for the demonstration. I was cordially greeted by Mr. Grimsley who introduced me to much of the COT Parks & Rec. staff who were there: Mr. Greg Bayor, Director; Mr. Brad Suder, Superintendent Planning, Design and Natural Resources Div.; Ms. Jessica Perez, Manager South Service Area; and Ms. Marsha Carter. There were also several other members of the COT Parks & Rec. staff present.

**The first display of the Truxor DM 5000 Aquatic Harvester
for demonstration at Bobby Hicks Lake, Tampa, FL
(Photo by Odie Jones, Jr., 19 Oct 12).**

I was very impressed at first sight of what I called an 'amphibious hyacinths excavator.' If you have ever been near or seen a piece of heavy equipment known as the 'caterpillar,' then that is what it reminded me of. Except, when I examined it closer, I could tell that it was much, much more than a mere piece of heavy equipment. Magnificent might be a good adjective to characterize such specialized machinery. I saw how easily it was maneuvered from its transport trailer to the ground using a sophisticated hydraulics control system. Then the operator smoothly drove it to the banks of the Bobby Hicks Park Lake on its tank-like tracks. Once out over the thick hyacinths, water paddles gave it the buoyancy needed to stay afloat. He first cleared a pathway for the harvester by using a basket-like metal scoop to separate and partially break up the plants. When that was done, the basket was replaced with a huge inverted rake to go beneath the hyacinths, lift them up and take them to the banks of the lake. Even though I expected it, I was pleased that I didn't see a huge cloud of black smoke billowing from the vehicle's surprisingly quiet 3-cylinders diesel engine.

The harvester goes beneath the hyacinths, breaks it apart and lifts it up before the operator transports it from Bobby Hicks Lake to shore (Photo by Odie Jones, Jr., 19 Oct 12).

This photo shows how the Truxor DM 5000 can be easily loaded and transported (Photo by Odie Jones, Jr., 19 Oct 12).

Although the demonstration didn't clear the lake in one day, just the sight of water being exposed in the small area which was cleared put a smile on my face and the faces of others witnessing the change take place. If we were asked to briefly assess the demonstration of the harvester, we would use single words like: operable, compact, strong, modern looking, versatile, efficient, supportable and economical. We know that there are much larger and more sophisticated machines on the market as advertised on the internet, but to even consider such vast undertakings might be *biting off more than we can chew.* We liked what we saw at the demonstration. We didn't know what accessories might be offered or planned for the vehicle which was displayed but we did understand the minimum process associated with this type of operation. Because this is one of the smaller harvesters, there could be at least three steps: (1) harvesting, (2) shredding, and (3) disposal. More than likely some hauling would also take place. We didn't want to "count our chickens before they hatched" but we thought it was okay to say thanks to those who had pitched in and a special THANK YOU to COT Parks & Rec. for their concerted efforts throughout.

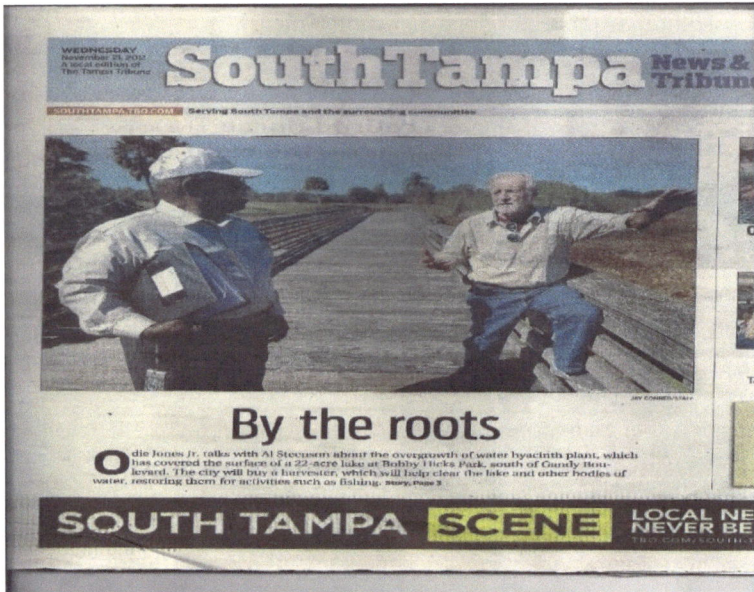

Tampa Tribune newspaper article "By the Roots," by Josh Poltillove announces the plans to purchase an aquatic plant harvester to rid Bobby Hicks Lake of hyacinths, 21 Nov 12.

The rest of the Trib story…"By the Roots," by Josh Poltilove which explains the use of a harvester to clear hyacinths out of Bobby Hicks Lake, Tampa, FL, 21 Nov 12.

The newspaper article was highly appreciated by the GCA and we expressed our thanks to Josh Poltilove with the following statement: "Thanks for the wonderful pictures and article titled "By the Roots," published in the South Tampa News & Tribune, Wednesday, Nov 21, 2012. Your interest in what happens here in Sun Bay South is a great tribute to the Gandy Civic Association, the Tampa Tribune, and the City of Tampa." The newspaper article helped to generate additional publicity for the Bobby Hicks Lake which seemed to have also revealed increased concern by responsible officials.

On December 15, 2012 Al sent me an email advising that purchase of the harvester had finally made the docket at Tampa City Council. The meeting had been scheduled for 9:00 a.m., December 20, 2012 and we had permission to speak before the council on behalf of the harvester. It was listed on the agenda as No. 24, File No. X2012-120, Resolution approving the "Single Source" proposal of Florida Aquatic Lake Management for the purchase of an Amphibious Machine in the estimated amount of $120,350 for use by the Parks and Recreation Department;

authorizing the Director of Purchasing to purchase said property,

supplies, materials or services.

This photo of Gadsden Park Lake was presented to Tampa
City Council to indicate GOOD!

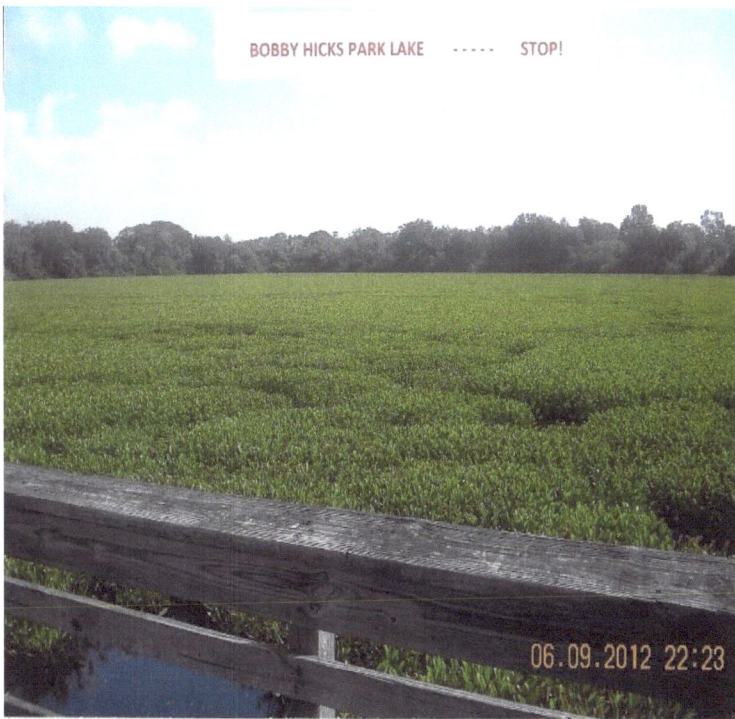

This photo of Bobby Hicks Park Lake was presented to Tampa City Council to indicate BAD!

Al and I arrived at Tampa City Council Chambers at City Hall on December 20, 2012 around 08:45 a.m. in preparation of the scheduled council meeting. I had a picture of the beautiful Gadsden Park Lake on which I wrote the word "GO" in green and a picture of the hyacinths covered Bobby Hicks Lake on which I wrote the word "STOP" in red. I placed the pictures on the photo viewer in succession so council members could get a clear view of them. I likened the GO and STOP to GOOD and

BAD. Al and I both told the council how desperate we were to get the lake cleaned out and we advised them to approve puchase of the harvester for the good of the entire COT. Not long after that the council voted unamimous approval of the resolution. We initially hoped to get the lake cleared out by Christmas after we learned it might be included in the Tampa 2013 fiscal budget. Realistically, we doubted it could happen that quickly. And, as expected, Santa Claus did not bring an amphibious machine in 2012.

The new year came and went while we waited and reminisced over how the lake used to look. There are photos of the Bobby Hicks Lake taken in November 2008 showing it to be crystal clear and unspoiled. It was our showpiece of pride and undaunted enjoyment as *big fish* tales were abounded. As reported previously by the GCA, this beautiful community treasure quickly disappeared beneath a blanket of invasive aquatic weed identified as water hyacinths.

We have been a part of several initiatives to revive the lake, but the most promising appeared to have surfaced when Mr. Bayor revealed the city's plan of action. The gist of that plan was mentioned in the Trib article, "By the roots." Josh wrote, "If all goes well, Bayor (COT Parks Director) anticipates the machine (harvester) will be bought and operating by Feb 1."

We considered February the month of great expectations. First, it had been almost one year since I took my first pictures of the overgrown lake. Second, we believed that COT Parks & Rec. would begin the cleanup in February. It was not too late. So we just awaited the word from Mr. Bayor who said once the harvester is purchased, Bobby Hicks Park Lake is first on the list. In our GCA report dated February 11, 2013, we expressed hopes of (COT Parks & Rec.) getting the harvester and beginning the huge task of clearing out the hyacinths during the month of February. Between those dates, we had what seemed like a standstill. Truth of the matter is the strong wheels of progress were still quietly turning, even though we couldn't see much movement. A momentous undertaking as with acquiring the technologically advanced machinery demanded careful coordination to achieve a positive outcome. This is how it should be when you are spending nonappropriated funds. It took initiative and resourcefulness to predict that this costly machine would do the job at hand and accrue dividends in the future. That responsibility is inherent with occupying a high position in government.

We at GCA weren't so naive to think we were getting our own harvester to be used only in Sun Bay South. Just to be sure GCA members understood this fully, President Steenson stated in the April 8, 2013 meeting, "Let's not deceive ourselves, we spoke highly in favor of the city purchasing the harvester, but that doesn't mean they won't use it for other projects." Although it wasn't broadcast daily, responsible city officials obviously had an agenda which included long range employment of the "big-ticket" item down the road after the Bobby Hicks Lake venture. For example, Mr. Bayor wrote in an email dated July 16, 2012 …"it would be helpful for all the city's lakes and ponds."

So, that day that we so anxiously looked forward to – getting the harvester, finally arrived. Mr. John Dellaquilla, Parks & Rec South Area Site Coordinator was trained and on the job. He had high hopes that the lake would be cleared sooner than many of us thought. He hoped to get two or three other operators trained on the harvester and planned to continue the process for at least four days a week. He was sure that once the lake was clear, it could be maintained in a useful condition. He said the fish were already there (and at least one alligator) and they would thrive in the 'new' lake.

Our hats were off to Mr. Dellaquilla and to others at COT Parks & Rec for their diligence and perseverance in landing the big fish – THE HARVESTER. The GCA and citizens of Sun Bay South community offered thanks to the COT and all who played a part in getting the machine. After that, we were compelled to patiently wait for the day when we would get our Bobby Hicks Lake back; with its cool, clear water and lots of fish.

We were very appreciative for the wonderful newspaper article, "Weed Machine Hard at Work," published by Staff Writer Elizabeth Behrman in the South Tampa Edition of the Tampa Tribune, May 16, 2013. She wrote:

"The city's newly acquired aquatic weed harvester has been put to work clearing out the lake at Bobby Hicks Park. The harvester uproots weeds and water hyacinth plants, and hauls them to land, where they dry completely before they are taken to an incinerator, said Greg Bayor, the city's parks and recreation director. The machine is also equipped with a basket to cleanup litter and other debris. The machine's manufacturer delivered the harvester, which cost more than $100,000, on May 7. The apparatus can clear about a half-acre of weeds daily, Bayor said. Once the machine is done with the 25-acre Bobby Hicks Lake, it will move to other lakes across the city. The plan is to operate the harvester four days a week, he said. Odie Jones, a member of the Gandy/Sun Bay South Civic Association, said neighborhood residents have rallied for years to get the lake cleaned up. When the weeds are cleared, people will be able to fish in the lake and use the pier again, he said. 'It shows that you care about the neighborhood when you keep things like that up so everybody can come in and enjoy it' Jones said."

This storage container was used to secure the harvester at night to aleviate transporting it daily. (Photo by Odie Jones, Jr., 7 May 13).

If you believe in Murphy's Quantum Law, then this is what it says: "Anything that can, could have or will go wrong, is going wrong, all at once. If there are two or more ways to do something, and one of those ways can result in a catastrophe or pregnancy, then someone will do it." Perhaps that is a slightly pessimistic viewpoint, but I will admit that it seems to be true on at least some occasions. For example, when we got the aquatic weed harvester, we crossed our fingers in hope that all would go well. Well, it did for a while and the lake was looking better each week as the COT Parks & Rec. staff worked hard to remove the hyacinths and allowed the long hidden water to come gleaming through to reflect the bright Florida sunlight.

Bobby Hicks Lake after removal of some of the hyacinths with the harvester. (Photo by Odie Jones, Jr., 10 Jun 13)

CHAPTER 9 -- LIKE THE TITANIC

As fate would have it, during the last week of June 2013, the harvester came to a dead stop and plunged into the deep like the Titanic. As I was informed, there was a malfunction and failure of a mechanical part which controls the buoyancy of the amphibious machine. It tilted out of control causing it to flip into the water. Luckily, the operator was able to jump from the vessel without being struck and was able to swim to shore. Not so fortunate for the expensive weed extractor; it submerged to the bottom of the pond, 3-cylinder engine and all. Obviously, the heated engine froze from the effects of the cool water which rendered it useless. We were told that a new engine and accessory parts were on order but the estimated time of arrival was undetermined. After all, the order had to come from Sweden and then through U.S. Customs. At least we could then see some water, even though the job was far from being finished. So in the meantime, I advised my neighbors to dig out their fishing gear, mosey on over to the Bobby Hicks Lake. Once there, we may as well pretend to *ice* fish if we can stand to look at the hyacinths that are still there.

On August 8, 2013, I sent an email to Mr. Grimsley requesting the status of the harvester. He called me Sunday, August 11 to advise that the parts ordered to repair the machine had been received. Preparations were ongoing to make the repairs and a transport trailer was being purchased. Because of the accident, a more in-depth training program would begin after the harvester was operational. He said he didn't think the hyacinths were spreading outward. Instead, they may appear to grow upward as the wind sweeps the floating plants from one area to another. It was estimated and hopeful that the lake would be cleared by the end of September, 2013. I told Mr. Grimsley that we had been considering the idea of sprucing up the Bobby Hicks Park with furniture; tables, benches, children's playground equipment, etc. He replied that there were no funds available for furniture at the time and he didn't think the Director COT Parks & Rec. would favor trying to get it into the budget. He also stated that new lawnmowers had been purchased and a new contract signed; therefore, the grass would be maintained in a better state in the future.

The guest speaker at the GCA monthly meeting on Monday, October 14, 2013 was none other than Tampa City Councilman Harry Cohen, District 4. One of his main talking points was the planned improvements for the Bobby Hicks Swimming Pool; which he said, included the Bobby Hicks Park. I called Ms. C Jo Ford, Legislative Aide to Councilman Cohen and left a message asking her to forward any written information her office had on the plans for improving the pool.

Mr. Grimsley called Tuesday, October 22 with an update on the harvester. As for the plan to make improvements to the pool, he believed those funds had been diverted to something else and it was unknown if the pool would be put back into the budget. The harvester had been repaired after receipt of the needed parts but as it was being taken out to begin the operator training, another problem developed. It was returned to the shop and another part was placed on order. As with the first parts, it would take weeks to receive that part and repair the harvester. Once the machine was fully operational, Mr. John Dellaquilla would likely be the trainer for several members of the COT Parks & Rec. staff. The blue container used to store the harvester at the lake was given up after the arrival of the new trailer. At any rate, Mr. Grimsley said he wanted to assure the GCA that they would continue working diligently to get the water hyacinths removed from the Bobby Hicks Lake as soon as possible.

When I talked to Mr. Grimsley on Monday, December 16, 2013, he seemed almost apologetic as he gave me an update on the harvester. It appeared to have fallen upon a bit of "bad luck" ever since its purchase less than a year ago. Who would have thought that the brand-new machine would fall in need of repair so much after finally making it all the way from overseas (Sweden) to the Bobby Hicks Park? Clearing out the annoying hyacinths seemed to have been going so smoothly for a while and then, everything came to a "splashing" stop as the harvester sank like the Titanic. What makes it even more perplexing is it was tested in a lake smaller than ours where again it began to falter after only a few days. Had it not been for sharp minds being thoughtful enough not to test it in the Bobby Hicks Lake, it might have ended up disabled in 11 to 19 feet of water mixed with thick hyacinths again. Instead, it was resting quietly in a repair shop awaiting a "control box" to be dispatched, slowly pass through U. S. Customs and arrive in Tampa before the next round of repairs. Ironically, the dispatch office is a continent away, in Europe and more precisely, in Sweden. Some pessimist might ask, "But doesn't everything coming into the U.S pass through Customs? It was estimated that the harvester could possibly be returned to finish up Bobby Hicks Lake in early February 2014. I could only say we should all stay positive, be optimistic and expect that the lake would eventually be restored fully to useful conditions.

Hyacinths in full bloom at Bobby Hicks Lake while the harvester is *'shopridden'*.
*(*Photo by Odie Jones, Jr., 8 May 14).**

**The Truxor being driven onto the new transport trailer
acquired by COT Parks & Rec.
(Photo by Odie Jones, Jr., 22 May 14).**

I wrote to Mr. Bayor on May 9, 2014 with courtesy copies to

Mr. John Grimsley and Mayor Bob Buckhorn. I told him that I

had visited the Bobby Hicks Park Lake on Thursday, May 8,

2014 and observed three teenage boys trying desperately to fish

in the lake. They attempted to remove some of the hyacinths by

hand to prevent it from snagging their fishing lines. I watched

them walk away with disappointment because they were unable

to catch the fish suspected of being in the lake. I explained to them the best I could that we would get the lake cleared of the weeds. I told Director Bayor that unfortunately, Al Steenson and I must explain to our Sunbay South/Gandy Civic Association members much too often that we were still trying to get the lake cleaned up. When I compare the Gadsden Park Lake just north of MacDill Air Force Base to our lake at Bobby Hicks Park, my eyes gradually tear-up. How could the Gadsden Park Lake be kept so beautiful and useful while the Bobby Hicks Lake remained in dire straits? These two parks and lakes were part of an aggressive renovation undertaking as early as the 1960s. As stated previously, over 15 years ago (Saturday, July 29, 2000) Mr. Orval Jackson of the Tampa Tribune wrote, "The parks department will be responsible for providing a road into the park, parking, removal of invasive plants and other improvement of conditions along the banks of the pond, restrooms, and overall maintenance." We've known since our initial effort to eradicate the hyacinths from the lake in May 2012 that it takes a cohesive team of contributors to get it done. We were enthusiastic about the prospects and rightfully so. We thought we were making huge strides when the Truxor was first demonstrated and purchased. Admittedly, we had little insight into the major tasks of research, procurement and funding of this complicated and expensive machine. It never occurred to us to ask someone if it was a machine manufactured and supported in the Continental United States. We applauded the efforts put forth by the COT and all departments involved but considering the number of maintenance setbacks with this vehicle, we were prompted to ask: Did the seller produce a dependable product? How far was the city required to go and what was the alternative? As we indicated above, getting the Bobby Hicks Lake cleared of the hyacinths was important to us and we were seeing the troublesome aquatic weed return in leaps and bounds. I asked Mr. Bayor to please tell us realistically when could we look forward to getting the lake cleared?

There was no doubt that Mr. Bayor was immensely serious in his efforts to get the harvester going and finalize the cleanup project. He was very prompt to reply to our email on May 12, 2014 with the following: "Working with new staff today to determine when the boat will be back in action. Should let you know something by Wednesday. As a reminder, last fall one of our operators unfortunately 'flipped' the weed harvester which caused severe electrical problems that has delayed the boat's activity for months; additionally, the initial training (the) staff took on the operations of the boat, obviously failed, which meant our Risk Management got involved and has developed an entire new set of training sessions that staff will be undergoing in the next few weeks. Given the photos you sent, it seems a sure bet we will be back to Bobby Hicks Lake shortly. Will let you know later this week." The next day, I received a phone call from Mr. Grimsley to say he also received our email to Mr. Bayor and he wanted to know if anybody had responded to it. He explained that he was not up to date on the status of the Truxor since he had been given new responsibilities for the indoor recreation portion of the department rather than the outside operations in the parks. He was very positive about the diligence of Coordinator John Dellaquilla in picking operators and upgrading the training scheme for the harvester after it was repaired. This was confirmed in a follow-up email from Mr. Bayor on May 15, 2014 which stated: "We have finalized who our most qualified operators will be, and will have them attend the new mandatory safety training either next week or the week after (not in our control as it's handled by Human Resources/Risk Management)." Mr. Bayor went on to say that upon completion of the training, Bobby Hicks Lake will be the first serviced. With that assurance, we sort of went about doing our own things and just letting Parks & Rec. take care of their business.

A crew of Truxor operators gathered for training (Photo by Odie Jones, Jr., 22 May 14).

On May 22, 2014, my wife and I were driving east on Manhattan Avenue when we saw a tent, several cars and a truck in the park near the lake. We could see that the truck had a trailer hitched to it but we couldn't tell much else. We wondered if it was a fishing party. After we returned home, there was nothing left to do except get my camera and proceed to Bobby Hicks Park. Upon my arrival, I was greeted by Mr. John Dellaquilla and seven other men. As I began to introduce myself, they all smiled and said, "Oh yes, we know who ODIE is. One of the gentlemen was operating the harvester out in the lake. Mr. Dellaquilla directed him to bring the machine onto shore. As it came out of the water and close to the tent we were all standing under, they began to chant "Odie, Odie, Odie" and pointed to the side of the now beautiful amphibious vehicle. Suddenly, I saw my name painted in big bold letters right there before my eyes and yet I could not believe what I saw. I could only ask, "What?" John explained that this was the result of my perseverance in trying to get the harvester in order to clear Bobby Hicks Lake of the weeds. I told him that I really appreciate the kind thought and I promise to continue trying until the job is done. Truth of the matter is I was totally astounded! I couldn't imagine ever having my name displayed on the side of that boat.

Though the name Odie was given to the harvester, it looked to be an ill-fated watercraft. (Photo by Odie Jones, Jr., 22 May 14).

This new crew of "hyacinth eradicators" was very hospitable to me. It was right around lunch time and I had sort of interrupted their semi-feast. Even though I had the good manners to say "No," they insisted that I have a sandwich and drink. The Cuban sandwich was delicious. Sherisha Hills arrived on the scene. We had the same things to say to each other: "It's a pleasure to finally meet you." She seemed quite consumed with the training of the seven operators who were now dedicated to this project to the end. Meaning: they wouldn't return to their original jobs until the lake was cleared. As Mr. Dellaquilla had explained to me earlier, classes started Tuesday, May 20th on the basic operations. Some actual operating of the machine took place Wednesday and Thursday. There were various stages of training taking place; starting and stopping the Truxor, taking it in and out of the water, loading it onto and off the trailer, and picking up the hyacinths and dumping it onto the shore. The written examination required each operator to get a minimum of 80% passing score. Just to be sure that I wasn't interfering with the training, I left the park.

Operator training to safely bring the hyacinths onto shore from the Bobby Hicks Lake. (Photo by Odie Jones, Jr., 22 May 14).

During that last visit to the lake, Mr. Dellaquilla informed me that the harvester had a worn alternator belt which meant they would have to take it to Fleet for replacement. After that, I was approached by several of our neighbors inquiring as to why they hadn't seen the harvester or crew cleaning out the lake any day during that following week. "Good question," I told them.

I telephoned Mr. Dellaquilla on Tuesday, June 3, 2014 to get an update. When I spoke with him he said he was trying to catch up on his paperwork. He explained that along with the alternator belt situation, they were mandated by Risk Management to acquire a water-proofed cellular phone for possible emergencies while operating the harvester. He said it would most likely be the second week of June before they would return to the lake.

I returned to the Park around noon on June 9, 2014 and it was all chained and locked up. I called Mr. Dellaquilla and he explained that he had just returned from attending his daughter's graduation. He also gave me a bit of new information. There was no vehicle dedicated to pull the trailer with the Truxor on board. He had been using his personal truck which he had to discontinue for various reasons, including not being rated for the heavy load, liability and safety. As soon as the transportation liaison got a proper vehicle, they would start harvesting again.

If you are superstitious, you may not believe in *good luck* on "Friday the Thirteenth." Mr. Dellaquilla had good news on Friday, June 13, 2014. He informed me that for sure he and his crew would have the harvester back in the lake removing the hyacinths. To me that was very good news.

Instead of the second week of June, it was then the end of the fourth week in August and the hyacinths were still growing like wild fire in a wind storm at the Bobby Hicks Lake. However, I did receive a telephone call from Mr. Dellaquilla on Friday, August 22, 2014 at 1:04 p.m. He said he was calling to update me on the status of the Truxor. He told me the machine had been back in operation since Tuesday, August 19 and had performed well since its repair. Again, he promised they would stick with it until the job was finished. One thing new was they had added another person to the staff whose full-time duties would be to help maintain and operate the harvester at Bobby Hicks Lake.

The status of the harvester seems to have again fallen into a state of limbo as of December 8, 2014. I tried to contact Ms. Sherisha Hill, South Team Supervisor but the phone still terminated at Mr. John Grimsley voice mail. I called the administrative office but reached a number which was no longer in service. When I called Mr. Dellaquilla, he explained that Ms. Hill had moved on to another job outside of the chain. The next person under the Director of Park & Rec. was Mr. Joe Green, Ground Maintenance Manager. Mr. Dellaquilla said he would have Mr. Green call me the next afternoon. I gathered from talking to Mr. Dellaquilla that there had been a problem with the cab stabilizer but things escalated to a point that the controller failed. It seemed nothing was being done until after they received a call from someone they thought was me. I venture to say it was our GCA President, Al Steenson who, as they say, 'Lit a fire under somebody' which changed priorities in the maintenance shop. After that call, the machine was practically disassembled with numerous parts all over the place. I was told that the parts distributor out of Miami was due to come to Tampa and assist with the repairs and he would be consulting with the Manufacturer in Sweden.

As promised by Mr. Dellaquilla, I received a telephone call from Mr. Green on December 9, 2014 in which he said he had been briefed and was fully aware of the maintenance problems associated with the harvester. He vowed to try to stay on top of the problem as much as he could; keeping in mind the vast new responsibilities his position carried.

It had been revealed back in September 2012 that some spraying of the lake was taking place and it wasn't just for mosquitos. This was stated outright by the amphibious boat operator I accosted. However, we suspect the herbicides being used weren't potent enough or not enough was being used to quickly kill the hyacinths. Based on conversation with Mr. John Grimsley it certainly appeared that he believed Hillsborough County Mosquito Control people were spraying the lake for control of the hyacinths. Evidence that something was happening to the hyacinths was showing up in photographs as early as January 2015.

A new view of water from the "Sonny" Bishop Pier with some hyacinths gone. (Photos by Odie Jones, Jr.).

Whenever you have high hopes of the success of a project, you are subject to view any news as good news. Because some Sun Bay South residents live in earshot of the Bobby Hicks Park, most have grown accustomed to listening for any sound resembling that of the engine of an aquatic harvester. After several anxious weeks of waiting for the Truxor to be repaired, many of us heard the roar of a commercial-like vehicle engine coming from the direction of the lake.

My visit to the lake that day revealed the program to eradicate the hyacinths from the Bobby Hicks Park Lake was still viable in spite of many setbacks. Maintenance of the harvester had been a huge problem for the COT Parks & Rec. from the beginning. Probably the most optimistic proponent of the vehicle, Mr. Dellaquilla told me at the time, he believed it was currently operating at 110% efficiency. He had complete faith that this machine would be able to finish the job. He assured me that the machine would not be used anywhere else until the Bobby Hicks Lake was cleared. One of the original "hyacinths eradicators" trained and assigned in June 2014 would continue to operate the machine for three days a week – Tuesday, Wednesday and

Thursday. However, rumor had it that there were plans to re-organize COT Parks & Rec. wherein caretaker for the Bobby Hicks Lake would be aligned under the COT Public Works Department. The change was expected to take place in about one month or so when additional Truxor operators would be dedicated to the completion of this project.

It appeared that an airboat crew from the FWC had been spraying the lake which was turning the weeds brown; after which some of the hyacinths died and sank to the bottom of the lake. President Al Steenson said he had talked to Mr. Thomas about it. Al told him, "This will make the harvesting easier but it could also create some damage to the lake." Mr. Thomas replied, "We know what we are doing and if necessary, we plan to re-stock the lake with fish afterwards.

CHAPTER 10 -- FWC TO THE RESCUE

After hearing the roar of an engine from an airboat on August 28, 2015, I proceeded over to the Bobby Hicks Lake where I witnessed the spraying of the lake. I just wanted to get a long overdue update of the cleanup of the hyacinths. I didn't know how the spraying had affected the cleanup -- but that was the only thing going on since a very long while. The word was going around that the Bobby Hicks Park was no longer the responsibility of Parks & Rec. but it had been transferred to the FWC.

While I was at the park, I met Mr. Joe Donavan, a concerned citizen who said he was at the park looking for a sign that the restoration of the lake had resumed. He shook his head and said,

"It's really a shame that they let the park and lake get into such bad shape. They should go over to Gadsden Park and see how nice that lake is kept and learn from it." I said, "True. But we are working on getting Bobby Hicks Park and Lake back up to par." He said, "Good Luck" as he walked away.

Bobby Hicks Lake coming to life after more hyacinths are submerged. (Photo by Odie Jones, Jr.).

Free from the hyacinths, the Bobby Hicks Lake looks alive and peaceful. (Photo by Odie Jones, Jr.).

During the month of September 2015, I heard of many sightings of water being seen in Bobby Hicks Lake. I mostly ignored the comments because several times before I had seen the lake with its decorative topping of the floral hyacinths spread throughout. I had not seen or heard the harvester, but several people told me that they had heard the roar of the airboat engine. I simply disregarded that as being HC Mosquito Control spraying to prevent the spread of Mosquitos. At the same time, I had seen a pickup truck drive down West Bay Avenue emitting a mist of spray from it. Besides, we had been promised long ago that the hyacinths would never be destroyed by spraying for fear of killing the lake. However, I couldn't ignore the fact that Mr. Thomas said they knew what they were doing in January 2015.

On September 15, 2015, Al sent Mr. Thomas an email inviting him to the next GCA meeting. In it he wrote, "Mr. Thomas: This will confirm our conversation today regarding your visit to the Gandy Civic Association to discuss the history and future of the Bobby Hicks Lake here in S. Tampa. Our next meeting will be held on October 12th @ 7:30 p.m. Our civic center is located at 4207 W. Oklahoma Ave., Tampa, FL 33616. As I mentioned, we have an A/V system which you can utilize. You merely have to bring your media. Please feel free to bring other folks that can share information with us. You will note that CC Mr. Odie Jones, he is our point man regarding this issue. We look forward to seeing you then. Should you have any questions, please feel free to contact me. Regards, Alan H. Steenson, President."

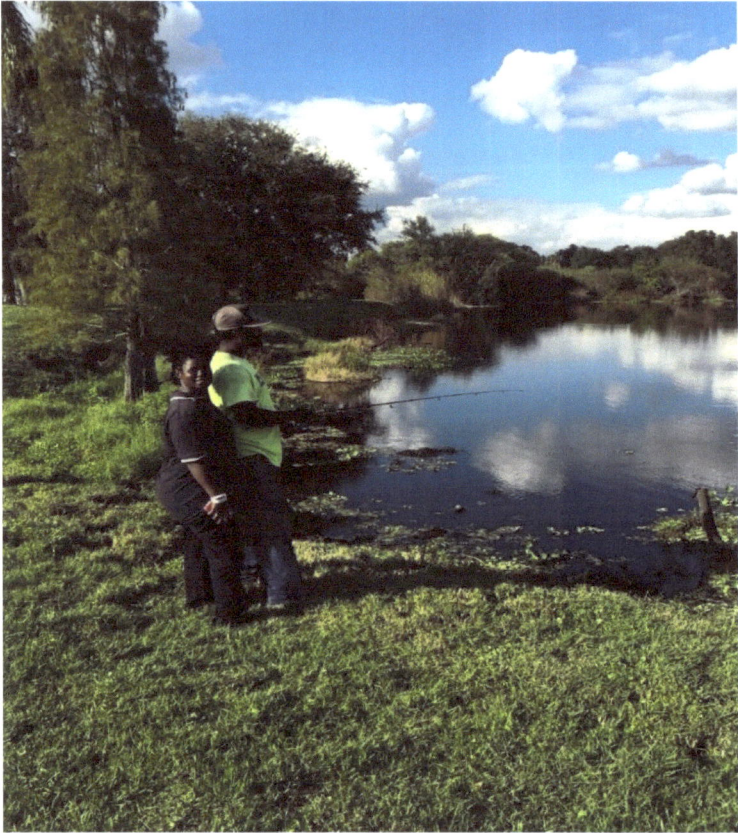

Kanesia and Angelo trying their luck in the hyacinth-free Bobby Hicks Lake. (Photo by Odie Jones, Jr., 8 Oct 15).

On October 8, 2015 I was driving along Mango Avenue when I noticed the gate to Bobby Hicks Park standing wide open. This, I thought, was my chance to get a close-up look at what was going on in the lake. When I reached the banks of the lake, I could not believe my own eyes. There stood a man and a woman fishing. I didn't know them, but they gave me the names Angelo and Kanesia. They allowed me to photograph them as they repeatedly threw their fishing line into the clear lake. They had not lost any fishing tackle to the unseen hyacinths but they hadn't caught any fish either. My question was, "Where did all the hyacinths go in such a brief period and did they (*the hyacinths*) take the fish with them?"

In the above photo, the Bobby Hicks Lake shows obvious signs of full recovery from the hyacinths.

We held our regular GCA meeting on October 12, 2015. The disappearance of the invasive weed had not been a mystery, but deliberate engineering by two professionals of the FWC. Mr. Paul Thomas is a Fisheries Biologist and Mr. Geoff Lokuta is an Invasive Plants Specialist. After the introductions by President Steenson, Mr. Thomas began by telling the group some history of the Fish Management Areas (FMAs); which includes Bobby Hicks Lake. The FMAs were established in 1998. An FMA is a pond, lake or other body of water established for the management of freshwater fish as a cooperative effort with the local county. The FWC Division of Freshwater Fisheries manages about 80 water bodies throughout the state that are designated as FMAs. Examples include most community-based fishing lakes and commission-managed impoundments. In many cases, these lakes are stocked with channel catfish, largemouth bass and sunshine bass. Automatic fish feeders and fish attractors concentrate sportfish for bank anglers. Hillsborough County is in the Southwest Region FWC Fish Management Area which includes: Al Lopez Park Lake (10 acres), Bobby Hicks Park Pond (25 acres), Dover District Park lake (14 acres), Gadsden

Park Pond (48 acres), Steven J. Wortham Park lake (10 acres) and Lake Thonotosassa (819 acres). It seemed important to note that out of the six bodies of water, only Gadsden Park and Bobby Hicks are called *ponds*. Some may call me dense but it just struck me like a bolt of lightning! PAUL W. THOMAS? Yep. That's him. The same Paul W. Thomas who was interviewed by Orval Jackson in 2000 and Jay Cridlin in 2002. Small world, isn't it?

Mr. Lokuta said he and Mr. Thomas had been made aware of the ongoing struggles by members of the GCA to rid the lake of the invasive vegetation. He thought the efforts by everyone should be commended but assured GCA members that FWC had been working the problem and have it well under control. Possibly the Bobby Hicks pond was not immediately on the high priority list for aquatic plant funding. We were anxious to learn if the designation 'pond' v. 'lake' had anything to do with the seemingly slow response to the hyacinth situation at Bobby Hicks Park. Perhaps the pond classification has ties to a statement made by Mr. Tom Ash, HCEPCH in an email dated June 11, 2012. He wrote, "the water quality in the pond, based on our sampling and laboratory analysis, is not remarkable and typical of an urban lake/pond that is being used for stormwater attenuation." The FWC has ten trust funds and a general revenue funding sources for FY 2015-2016. Out of a total budget of $357,395,953, the Invasive Plant Control Trust Fund is only $8,456,298; the fourth smallest.

The visit by Mr. Thomas and Mr. Lokuta prompted us to research the Programs of the FWC 2015-2016. We found the following information on the internet:

(1) The Division of Habitat & Species Conservation, Invasive Plant Management section is responsible for directing, coordinating and funding two statewide programs controlling invasive upland plants on public conservation lands and invasive aquatic plants in public waterways. It regulates, through a permitting program, projects for control of aquatic plants that do not meet the eligibility requirements for state funding. The FWC protects Florida's native plant and wildlife diversity through the management of invasive plants on public lands and waterways; dissemination of information;

public education efforts; contractual research; and surveillance of plant communities on public lands and waterways. This section's goal is to protect native fish and wildlife habitat by reducing existing populations of invasive plants and preventing new invasive plant populations from becoming established.

(2) The Division of Freshwater Fisheries Management, Hatchery Operations and Stocking – The state has two freshwater hatcheries: the Florida Bass Conservation Center at Richloam Hatchery and the Blackwater Fisheries Research and Development Center. They produce a dependable quantity of size-specific, high quality freshwater fish, which are stocked annually in more than 200 Florida lakes, rivers and community-managed waters.

We also discovered on the internet that there are three reasons to consider stocking: (1) the pond is new with no fish population; (2) undesirable species have invaded the pond; or (3) an established fish population has reached an unbalanced state where prey species (bream) have overpopulated and interfered with predator (bass) reproduction, or vice-versa. Fish stocking is an important part of any management program. The choice of fish to stock depends on the lake owner's goals and size of the body of water. Large lakes may be hard to manage, but it is also difficult to manage a pond of less than one-acre for species such as bass and bluegill. The most common strategy for pond and lake stocking is to combine largemouth bass and bluegill (and/or redear sunfish). The combination of bass and bluegill generally works well in lakes larger than one-acre and provides excellent fishing for both species indefinitely because of their relationship. The best part of the bass and bluegill lake system is its simplicity. In a well-functioning pond, phytoplankton, zooplankton, and insect larvae will be abundant enough to supply food for bass fry and all sorts of bluegill. The bluegill will reproduce and grow rapidly with the abundant food and provide excellent forage for bass. As long as bass are not over-harvested, they will keep bluegill from overpopulating. However, some large bluegill will survive bass predation and in turn provide excellent bluegill angling.

A WARNING ALLIGATORS sign at Bobby Hicks Lake, Tampa, FL.

Mrs. Alligator says, "When I let you go, remember this is gator country!"

Alligators are migratory at times and will find your pond sooner or later. Both sexes become sexually mature when they attain a length of 6 to 7 feet. They are not normally aggressive toward humans, but aberrant when fed by humans. Their presence is of little concern unless they lose their fear of humans. Feeding alligators is dangerous and strictly prohibited by state and federal laws. Several adult alligators have been spotted in the Bobby Hicks Lake. Two had to be removed due to aggressive behavior toward each other. They do not affect recreational fisheries. If you observe an alligator more than 4 feet long that displays bold or aggressive behavior, call the FWC Alligator Hotline 1-866-FWC-Gator (392-4286) to request its removal.

EPILOGUE

Our wish list for the Bobby Hicks Park is still long and wanting, and has been ever since Mr. Paul Thomas expressed the brilliant plans on behalf of the COT Parks & Rec. Dept. in 2000. The removal of hyacinths along with providing a road, parking and restrooms was clearly spelled out back then. In May 2014, I mentioned furnishings for the Park to Mr. Dellaquilla. I was surprised to learn from him that there were already benches in storage at Port Tampa and they planned to install them after the hyacinths were cleared from the lake. He said the benches had been removed previously because of vandalism (set afire, etc.) by druggies and others.

While the harvester was in and out of the shop, we had lots of time to plan for the park as well as the lake. This was despite what Mr. Grimsley had said about the sparsity of funds. As with any venture, accessibility must rank high on the list. For example, the Gadsden Park has a concrete walking/jogging trail surrounding it. The Bobby Hicks Park is only accessible from the East side; the South side is blocked by a drainage ditch and the North and West sides are inundated with overgrown brush and a drop-off shoreline. Along with not being user-friendly, there has been little to attract Sun Bay South residents as well as visitors to the area.

Perhaps the inattentiveness to the boundary of the lake is attributed to the overwhelming invasion of the hyacinths. The fence on the North and West sides is somewhat of an obstruction but that shouldn't stop a usefulness and beautification effort. Because of the drop-off shoreline on the North and West sides of the lake, some filling would most likely need to be done. A driveway and parking lot should be established on the Southeast side of the park for easy access by everyone. And of course, the establishment of restrooms and accessability for the handicapped persons is a must.

Sometimes we will go far away seeking a solution to a difficult problem when later we learn that the answer is just around the corner. We had a most demanding situation with the invasive hyacinths in the Bobby Hicks Lake and after some thought and deliberations we chose to reach out to a Truxor builder overseas in Sweden to get an aquatic harvester. Our hope was that the intricate machine would clear the lake in a matter of months. But as fate would have it, the lake was expansive and probably too deep for a harvester that small. Too, the hyacinths were thick and most resilient – they sprang back overnight as with a vengeance. As it turned out, the FWC out of nearby Lakeland, FL had the knowledge and experience to eliminate the pesky weeds in a matter of a few months just by spraying the lake. Granted, it may take a few years before we can again have the pleasure of catching the *big fish* at Bobby Hicks Park Lake, but we will gladly live with that circumstance.

The latest word on the Truxor aquatic harvester named "Odie" is it is repaired and in full use. The maintenance crew learned the mechanics of keeping it afloat and a crew of operators are well trained in its maneuverability. Several of the previously unkept ponds and streams about Tampa are now gleaming with beauty thanks to the 'big ticket' machine.

ABOUT THE AUTHOR

ODIE JONES, JR. is a graduate of Summerville High School, Aliceville, Alabama where he also earned the honor of Class Salutatorian. Jones retired from the U.S. Air Force June 1, 1984 after serving for twenty-eight years and attaining the rank of Senior Master Sergeant. He had numerous military assignments both in the U.S. and overseas; including one year in the Vietnam War. He received twenty-one prestigious awards and medals during his career. He is listed in the 2012 AF Memorial Registry and received the 2012 Airman's Society Certificate of Recognition.

As a charter member of the Bay Area Brotherhood, a nonprofit veteran's civic organization in Tampa, Florida, Jones has held the office of Treasurer, Secretary, Vice President and President multiple terms. He is the club's historian and primary writer. He is a life member of the Joint Communications Support Element Veterans Association and Vice President of the Gandy Civic Association, both in Tampa, FL. He briefly attended the University of Tampa, Tampa, FL.

Odie has written numerous articles for military command publications and news releases for commercial newspapers. He is currently in the process of publishing the first of four books he has authored.

BIBLIOGRAPHY

Lake and Reservoir Management: Practical Applications, North American Lake Management Society, McAfee, NJ, 1985.

Florida Fish and Wildlife Conservation Commission (FWC) Fish Management Areas, State of Florida, 1999-2016.

Bobby Hicks Park Renovation to Hook Families on Fishing, The Tampa Tribune, 2000.

Club Hooks Fishing Pier for Park, St. Petersburg Times, 2002.

Bobby Hicks Park, Tampa, FL | Flikr - Photo Sharing! (2009).

Water Hyacinth, Wikipedia, the free encyclopedia (2012).

Robinson Lake, email, Mrs. Laura Roake, 2012.

Environment Petition: Clean Up Bobby Hicks Pond, Ms. Tracy Norman, 2012.

In Tampa, Parks Make the City, Tampa Bay Times, 2012.

Bobby Hicks Lake, email, Mr. Greg Bayor, Director City of Tampa Parks and Recreation Department, 2012.

By the Roots, South Tampa/Central Tampa News & Tribune, 2012.

The Tampa City Council, Regular Final Agenda, 12/20/2012.

Aquatic Weed Harvester Clearing Lake at Bobby Hicks Park, 2013.

Aquatic Plant Management – Mechanical Harvesting, Department of Ecology, State of Washington.

Plant Management in Florida Waters: An Integrated Approach, Florida Department of Environmental Protection (DEP).

INTENTIONALLY BLANK

www.ingramcontent.com/pod-product-compliance
Lightning Source LLC
Chambersburg PA
CBHW040513290326
41930CB00036B/110